Christmas Instruments In Praise

ARRANGED BY LLOYD LARSON

MELODY OR HARMONY FOR SOLO OR DUET
PERFORMANCE WITH ANY OTHER BOOK IN THIS SERIES

BG0962A - Accompanist Edition (works with *all* solo editions)
BG0962B - B♭ Edition (for Trumpet, Clarinet, Baritone [𝄞], Tenor Saxophone)
BG0962C - C Edition (for Flute, Violin, Oboe)
BG0962D - Bass Clef Edition (for Trombone, Cello, Baritone [𝄢], Bass Violin)
BG0962E - E♭ Edition (for Alto Saxophone, English Horn)
BG0962F - F Edition (for French Horn)
BG0962G - Alto Clef Edition (for Viola)

Music engraving by Dick Bolks.

How Best to Use These Books

This *Instrumental Praise & Worship* series of books, together with our two other instrumental series, *Sacred Songs for Instruments*, and *Instruments In Praise*, seem to fill a strong need of beginning players looking for solo material they might use for lessons, and then ultimately be able to use in a church service. Then there are others who might not want to play solo, but who would be willing to play the second part of a duet. Our instrumental books are a good solution to that particular situation: each contains a solo line *and* a duet line. The included eight-page supplement is a transposition of the melody, in big notes; and optional harmony, in cue-sized notes. The *notes* are the same for all editions, but they have been properly scored for the respective instruments. Now it is possible to play the melody on a flute using the C edition, and the harmony played on a sax using the E♭ book. This flexibility greatly increases the usability of all of our instrumental publications.

Accompanists take note: on the Piano Accompaniment part, the melody is written in cue-sized notes above the treble clef. Let the soloist(s) take the lead. You *accompany*! Work together as a team. Play well, accompanist; play well soloist I; and play well, soloist II! I hope using these will be great fun for everyone.

Instrumentalists take note: we recommend playing selected phrases of the solo part up or down an octave, as best suits the comfort and level of each individual performer.

Take a look at our other instrumental publications . . .

Sacred Songs for Instruments B♭ (BG0580); C (BG0581); Bass Clef (BG0582); E♭ (BG0583).
Arranged by Fred Bock
This series, for solo and/or duet instrumental presentation includes: *Blessed Assurance; Eternal Father, Strong to Save; Great Is Thy Faithfulness; His Eye Is On the Sparrow; How Great Thou Art; Oh, I Never Shall Forget the Day; Safe In the Arms of Jesus; Save, Saved!; Softly and Tenderly; Swing Low, Sweet Chariot; The Savior Is Waiting; Thou Art Worthy; To God Be the Glory; Up From the Grave He Arose; What a Wonderful Savior.* (Easy to medium-easy difficulty)

Instruments In Praise B♭ (BG0725); C (BG0726); Bass Clef (BG0727); E♭ (BG0728).
Arranged by Lloyd Larson
This series, also for solo and/or duet presentation, includes: *Come, Thou Fount; Come, We That Love the Lord; Day by Day, and With Each Passing Moment; Deep River; Guide Me, O Thou Great Jehovah; Savior, Like a Shepherd, Lead Us; Spirit Of God, Descend Upon My Heart; Stand Up, Stand Up for Jesus.* (Medium difficulty)

Instrumental Praise & Worship B♭ (BG0924); C (BG0925); Bass Clef (BG0926); E♭ (BG0927).
Arranged by Fred Bock
This series, for solo and/or duet presentation, includes: *As the Deer; Give Thanks; He Is Exalted; He Is Lord; His Name Is Wonderful; How Majestic Is Your Name; I Love You, Lord; I Will Call Upon the Lord; In my Life, Lord, Be Glorified; Jesus, Name Above All Names; Majesty; Our God Reigns; Seek Ye First the Kingdom of God; Thou Art Worthy; We Have Come Into His House.* (Medium Difficulty)

IT CAME UPON THE MIDNIGHT CLEAR

RICHARD S. WILLIS
Arranged by LLOYD LARSON

O COME, ALL YE FAITHFUL

JOHN F. WADE
Incorporating FOR UNTO US A CHILD IS BORN
by GEORGE F. HANDEL
Arranged by LLOYD LARSON

AWAY IN A MANGER

*Incorporating CRADLE SONG
by WILLIAM J. KIRKPATRICK
and AWAY IN A MANGER
by JAMES R. MURRAY
Arranged by LLOYD LARSON*

REJOICE AND SING NOEL!

ALLAN ROBERT PETKER
Arranged by LLOYD LARSON

GO, TELL IT ON THE MOUNTAIN

TRADITIONAL SPIRITUAL
Arranged by LLOYD LARSON

GENTLE MARY LAID HER CHILD

TEMPUS ADEST FLORIDUM
(Piae Cantiones, 1582)
Arranged by LLOYD LARSON

ON CHRISTMAS NIGHT ALL CHRISTIANS SING

TRADITIONAL ENGLISH CAROL
Arranged by LLOYD LARSON

(no rit. to end)

WE THREE KINGS OF ORIENT ARE

JOHN H. HOPKINS, JR.
Arranged by LLOYD LARSON